The Exemplar and Role Model for Mankind

Imam al-Kazim

By:

The Religious Authority

Grand Ayatollah al-Sayyid Mohammed Taqi al-Modarresi

Translated by Household Publications

MW01441535

بسم الله الرحمن الرحيم

In the Name of Allah, the Compassionate the Merciful

Contents

Introduction 9
Chapter One: The Noble Origin and Blessed Birth 11
His Parents: 15
His Attributes: 15
His Upbringing: 15
Chapter Two: The Imam and His Era 21
The Era of Imam Mūsā b. Jaʿfar (peace be upon him): 23
The Era of Hārūn al-Rashīd: The Peak of Abbasid Terrorism: 26
The Ordeal of the Alawi House: 27
The Story of ʿUbaidullah al-Bazzāz al-Nīshābūrī 28
The Difficult Circumstances Facing Scholars 30
Infiltrating the Abbasid Government 31
A) The Story of the "Robe" 34
B) Secret Communications 35
C) Taqiyya Even in Wuḍū 36
Chapter Three: The Miracles an d Knowledge of Imam al-Kāẓim (a) ... 41
The Miracles of Imam al-Kāẓim: 43
The Knowledge of the Imamate 51
Chapter Four: His Character and Virtues 59
His Character and Virtues: 61
A) His Worship and Asceticism: 62

In the Name of Allah, the Compassionate the Merciful

All praise belongs to Allah, the Lord of the worlds, the All-beneficent, the All-merciful, Master of the Day of Retribution. You [alone] do we worship, and to You [alone] do we turn for help. Guide us on the straight path, the path of those upon whom You have bestowed favors. Not (the path) of those upon whom Your wrath is brought down, nor of those who go astray.

Introduction

Praise be to Allah, and peace upon His chosen servants, Muḥammad and his noble household.

At a time when the world is witnessing a genuine Islamic revival, becoming a hope for the hearts of the deprived and a threat to the existence of the oppressors, the arrogant powers and oppressors of the world are devising plans to either block this wave or at least contain it, and their demons whisper in their ears that nothing else will corrupt this nation except what corrupted its beginning, which is sowing the sectarian seed, establishing systems of tyranny and oppression in the name of religion, and reviving the spirit of pre-Islamic tribalism.

Thus, mercenary pens strike the chord of sectarianism, attacking the school of thought of the Ahl al-Bayt, and continually repeat the phrase "Shiite terrorism," hoping to stir deep-seated Umayyad hatreds in some Muslims.

In this context, it is imperative for honorable pens and clean consciences to rise to the duty of preserving the gains of the nation and protecting the sources of the new Islamic revival from the filth of devils, their incantations, whispers, and misleading media.

Let us cast aside ignorant tribalism, defend Allah's messages, His great messengers, peace be upon them, and the Messenger of Allah, Muḥammad b. ʿAbdullah, peace be upon him and his family, and his oppressed household, peace be upon them, and the genuine prophetic path in the nation.

Verily, Satan has mustered his forces to come to you with his cavalry and infantry, having prepared all his tricks and traps to mislead you and divert you from the right path. Let us arm ourselves with increased awareness, be extremely cautious, and use our pens as shields to defend the sanctities of the nation, the household of the Prophet, and their righteous path in resisting the regimes of hypocrisy that are reemerging today.

I see clearly that focusing on the heritage of the Ahl al-Bayt, represented in their approach, biography, their explanation of Quranic knowledge, and their interpretation of the Prophet's Sunnah ensures the continuity, integrity, and victory of the Islamic revolution by Allah's will. Neglecting this matter would be a grave mistake.

On the twenty-fifth day of Shawwal in the year 1405 AH, which coincides with the anniversary of the martyrdom of Imam al-Ṣādiq, peace be upon him, I begin writing a new part of the series *Exemplar and Role Models* recounting the life of the son of Imam al-Ṣādiq, Imam Mūsā b. Jaʿfar, peace be upon him, whose life is full of lessons and revolutionary teachings.

I consider this a modest contribution to counter the conspiracies of the arrogant against the path of the Ahlul Bayt, peace be upon them, and their deceit in containing the genuine Islamic revival. I ask Allah Almighty to grant me success in completing this part and the other parts of the series, and to benefit me with it on the day when neither wealth nor children will benefit except those who come to Allah with a sound heart.

Chapter One

The Noble Origin and Blessed Birth

It appears that the village of al-Abwāʾ, located between Medina and Mecca, often attracted the pilgrimage caravans of the Ahl al-Bayt more than others, as it was the resting place of the Prophet's mother, Amina bint Wahab.

On their way back to Medina after performing Hajj at the Kaʿba[1], the caravan of Imam Abū ʿAbdullah al-Ṣādiq, peace be upon him, stopped in this village on the seventeenth of Ṣafar in the year 128 AH, according to the most renowned narrations. The Imam was hosting his guests with a meal when a messenger came from his wives to give him the glad tidings of the blessed newborn.

A historical narration by al-Manhāl al-Qaṣṣāb states: "I left Mecca intending to go to Medina, and I passed by al-Abwāʾ, where a son was born to Abū ʿAbdullah (Imam al-Ṣādiq), peace be upon him. I reached Medina before him, and he arrived a day later, feeding people for three days. I was among those who ate, and I would eat nothing until the next day, returning to eat again. I did this for three days, eating until I was satisfied, then eating nothing until the next day."

Another hadith narrated by Abū Baṣīr says: "I was with Abū ʿAbdullah (al-Ṣādiq), peace be upon him, in the year his son Mūsā was born. When we stopped at al-Abwāʾ, Imam al-Ṣādiq, peace be upon him, prepared lunch for us and his companions, making it plentiful and delicious. While we were eating, a messenger came from Ḥamīda, saying: 'The labor pains have started, and you yourself ordered me to inform you of this matter, that this child is not like other children.'

---

1. See: *Biḥār al-Anwār,* vol. 48, p. 4, and also *al-Maḥāsin* by al-Barqī, vol. 2, p. 418.

Imam al-Ṣādiq, peace be upon him, rose up happy and joyful and it was not long before he returned to us with his sleeves rolled up and a smile on his face. We said: 'May Allah make you smile forever and bring joy to your eyes. What did Hamīda do?' He replied: 'Allah has given me a boy who is the best creation of Allah. She told me something about him that I knew better than she did.'

I asked: 'May I be sacrificed for you! What did Ḥamīda tell you about him?' He said: 'She said that when he was born, he placed his hands on the ground and lifted his head towards the sky. I told her that this is a sign of the Messenger of Allah, peace be upon him and his family, and a sign of the Imam after him.'

I asked: 'May I be sacrificed for you! What is the sign of the Imam?'

He said: 'On the night my grandfather was conceived, an angel came to my great-grandfather while he was asleep, bringing him a cup containing a drink thinner than water, whiter than milk, softer than butter, sweeter than honey, and colder than snow. The angel gave it to him and ordered him to drink it, then to engage in intercourse. My great-grandfather woke up joyfully and did so, resulting in the conception of my grandfather. On the night my father was conceived, an angel came to my grandfather in the same manner, giving him the drink and ordering him to drink and engage in intercourse. My grandfather woke up joyfully and did so, resulting in the conception of my father. On the night I was conceived, an angel came to my father, giving him the drink and ordering him to do the same. My father woke up joyfully, aware of Allah's will for me, and did so, resulting in my conception. On the night this son of mine was conceived, an angel came to me as he had come to my great-grandfather, my grandfather, and my father, giving me the drink and ordering me as he had ordered them. I woke up joyfully, aware of Allah's will for me, and did so, resulting in my son's conception. Here he is, by Allah, your leader after me.'"[1]

---

1. *Biḥār al-Anwār,* vol. 48, p.2.

When the Imam returned to Medina, he fed the people for three days, and they rejoiced at the birth of the blessed child.

His Parents:

Father: The Imam of Guidance, Abū ʿAbdullah Jaʿfar b. Muḥammad al-Ṣādiq, peace be upon him.

Mother: Hamīda al-Barbariyya, who might have been from Andalusia or Morocco, and was nicknamed Ḥamīda al-Muṣaffāt (Hamīda the Purified).

Hamīda was among the most virtuous women, undertaking the mission of spreading the message, and she narrated some hadiths from her husband. Ibn Sinān narrates from Sābiq b. al-Walīd, and he reports from al-Muʿallā b. Khunays who reported that Abū ʿAbdullah (peace be upon him) said: "Hamīda is purified from impurities like a refined ingot of gold. Angels have constantly guarded her until she was brought to me as an honor from Allah for me and the proof after me."[1]

His Attributes:

His personal features reflected his great soul and the immense responsibility he had to fulfill. He was a noble Hashimite with bright features, a square build, dark complexion, and a thick beard, exuding awe and majesty.

His titles reveal the prophetic qualities that manifested in him: al-Kāẓim (the one who suppresses anger), al-Ṣābir (the patient one), al-Ṣālih (the righteous one), and al-Amīn (the trustworthy one). Indeed, his life was full of manifestations of these virtuous qualities.

His Upbringing:

For twenty years of his noble life, his father, Imam Abū ʿAbdullah

---

1. *Biḥār al-Anwār,* p. 6, cited from *al-Kāfī,* vol. 1, p. 477.

al-Ṣādiq (peace be upon him), nurtured him, pointing out his virtues and explaining to his closest followers that he (Imam Mūsā al-Kāẓim) was the master of his sons and the Imam after him.

The Imamate must be explicitly appointed, and the texts about the twelve Imams from the Prophet Muḥammad (peace be upon him and his family) have been transmitted uninterruptedly and continuously. Every Imam would appoint his successor, and thus, the followers of the Ahl al-Bayt (peace be upon them) were keen to know their Imam, asking the predecessor about the successor.

Abd al-Raḥmān b. al-Ḥajjāj narrates:

"I entered upon Jaʿfar b. Muḥammad in his house, and he was in in a certain room in his mosque, praying, with Mūsā b. Jaʿfar (peace be upon him) on his right, saying 'Āmeen' to his supplication. I said to him: 'May Allah make me your ransom! You know my dedication to you and my service to you. Who is the person in charge of the affair after you?' He said: 'O Abd al-Rahman! Mūsā has worn the armor, and it has fit him.' I said: 'I do not need anything after this.'"[1]

Imam al-Ṣādiq (peace be upon him) would advise his other sons about the right of his son Mūsā (peace be upon him). To his older son, ʿAbdullah, he said:

"What prevents you from becoming like your brother? By Allah, I see the light in his face." ʿAbdullah replied: "How so? Is my father and his father not the same? Is my origin and his origin not the same?" Abū ʿAbdullah said to him: "He is from my soul, and you are my son."[2]

The life of Imam Mūsā (peace be upon him) was distinguished from childhood, indicating his great status. It is narrated from Ṣafwān al-Jammal, one of the special Shiites:

"I asked Imam Jaʿfar al-Ṣādiq (peace be upon him) about the owner

---

1. *Biḥār al-Anwār,* vol. 48, p. 181.

2. Ibid., p. 18.

of this matter (i.e. the one who in charge of Imamate). He said: 'The owner of this matter is one who does not engage in idle play or amusement.' At that moment, Abū al-Ḥassan (Imam Mūsā Al-Kāẓim), who was still a child, entered with a lamb and a goat that had not yet reached its first year. Abū al-Ḥassan was saying to the lamb: "Prostrate to your Lord." So, Imam al-Ṣādiq embraced him and said: "May my father and mother be sacrificed for the one who does not engage in idle play or amusement."' [1]

Thus, Mūsā b. Jaʿfar grew up beloved among his brothers because of his distinct characteristics and following his father's advice regarding him. Among his steadfast followers was ʿAlī b. Jaʿfar. It is narrated from Muḥammad b. al-Walid:

"I heard ʿAlī b. Jaʿfar b. Muḥammad al-Ṣādiq say: 'I heard my father Jaʿfar b. Muḥammad (peace be upon him) say to a group of his special companions: "Be good to my son Mūsā, for he is the best of my children and the one I leave behind after me. He is my successor and the proof of Allah upon all His creation after me."

ʿAlī b. Jaʿfar was very devoted to his brother Mūsā, adhering closely to him, taking religious teachings from him, and had many famous questions and answers narrated from him directly. The narrations on this are too numerous to count as we have described and outlined.'"[2]

Since the era of Imam al-Ṣādiq (peace be upon him) was marked by some relief, the teachings of the Ahl al-Bayt spread, and their school of thought became one of the most widespread and followed in the Islamic world. The fear for the future of the religion of Ahl al-Bayt (peace be upon them) was genuinely intense inasmuch as some leaders were likely to covet the leadership of the denomination, and perhaps some of Imam al-Ṣādiq's children or grandchildren might be drawn to them. Therefore, the Imam's emphasis that his successor was his son

1. Ibid., p. 19.
2. Ibid., p. 20.

Mūsā (peace be upon him) was strong and continuous.

That was why some people deviated, claiming that the guardian after Imam al-Ṣādiq (peace be upon him) was his elder son Ismāʿīl, saying he did not die during his father's lifetime but rather disappeared from sight. The Ismāʿīlī sect, which founded a great revolutionary movement after the prophetic mission and built a vast state in North Africa, was born from this incorrect notion.

For this reason, Imam al-Ṣādiq (peace be upon him) made his senior Shiites witness the death of his son and confirmed to them that the rightful successor after him was Mūsā (peace be upon him), not anyone else.

It is narrated from Zurāra b. Aʿyan:

"I entered upon Abū ʿAbdullah (peace be upon him) and to his right was the master of his children, Mūsā (peace be upon him), and before him was a covered coffin. He said to me: 'O Zurāra! Bring me Dāwūd al-Raqqī, Ḥumran, and Abū Baṣīr.' Al-Mufaḍḍal b. ʿUmar entered upon him, and I went out and brought those whom he had ordered me to bring. People continued to enter one after another until we were thirty men in the house. When the gathering was complete, he said: 'O Dāwūd! Uncover Ismāʿīl's face for me.' I uncovered his face, and Imam Jaʿfar al-Ṣādiq (peace be upon him) said: 'O Dāwūd! Is he alive or dead?' Dāwūd replied: 'My master, he is dead.' He asked each person individually, and they all said: 'He is dead, my master.' He said: 'O Allah, bear witness.' Then he ordered his washing, embalming, and shrouding.

When he was done, he said to al-Mufaḍḍal: 'Uncover his face for me.' Al-Mufaḍḍal uncovered his face and said: 'Is he alive or dead?' Al-Mufaḍḍal said: 'Dead.' Abū ʿAbdullah said: 'O Allah, bear witness upon them.'

He was then carried to his grave. When he was placed in his niche, Abū ʿAbdullah said: 'O Mufaḍḍal, uncover his face.' He asked the group: 'Is he alive or dead?' We said: 'He is dead.' He said: 'O Allah, bear witness and let them bear witness, for the wrongdoers will doubt, ‘**wanting to extinguish the light of Allah with their mouths**.' Then he pointed to Mūsā (peace be upon him) and said: **'By Allah, Allah will complete His light even if the disbelievers detest it.'**[1] Then they covered him with earth. He then repeated to us: 'The deceased, shrouded, embalmed, and buried in this grave, who is he?' We said: 'Ismāʿīl.' He said: 'O Allah, bear witness.' He then took Mūsā's hand and said: 'He is the truth, and the truth is with him and will remain with him until Allah inherits the earth and those upon it.'"[2]

1. Quran, 61: 8 -9.
2. *Biḥār al-Anwār,* vol. 48, p. 21.

Chapter Two

The Imam and His Era

The Era of Imam Mūsā b. Jaʿfar (peace be upon him):

The duration of the Imamate of Al-Kāẓim (peace be upon him) was thirty-five years. He undertook it from the age of twenty in 148 AH until his martyrdom in 183 AH, at the age of fifty-five.

During this time, he witnessed the end of the rule of al-Manṣūr, the reign of al-Mahdī for ten years, al-Hādī for one year, and Hārūn al-Rashīd for fifteen years. The Abbasid rule was at its strongest during this period, so much so that the era of al-Rashīd is often referred to as the golden age. Undoubtedly, the strength of the Islamic state during this era cannot be compared to other times. Simultaneously, the revolutionary movement had gained significant strength during the time of Imam Al-Kāẓim (peace be upon him), positioning him to lead a comprehensive revolution if it had not been for certain circumstances that prevented its outbreak and delayed its success.

The conflict between the Abbasid authority and the revolutionary movement reached its peak during the reign of al-Rashīd. From various historical texts and events, we can deduce that the revolutionary plan was ready, and the Abbasid authority failed to contain the movement even during its golden age. This was because the supporters of the revolutionary movement had increased, not just among the people but also among some senior state officials who leaned towards the movement to some extent. This possibly explains the attempt of Maʾmūn, the Abbasid Caliph, to draw closer to the Alawite house, especially Imam ʿAlī b. Mūsā al-Riḍā (peace be upon him), whose father was killed by al-Rashīd. The incidents that guide us to this truth are as follows:

There are some narrations indicating that it was destined for the seventh Imam to take on the matter, and it became well-known among the Shīʿa that he is the Qāʾim[1] from the family of Muḥammad (peace be upon him and his family), who will not die until Allah, through him, fills the earth with justice after it has been filled with tyranny and injustice.

For instance, Abū Ḥamza al-Thumālī reported that he said to Abū Jaʿfar, Imam al-Bāqir (peace be upon him): "ʿAlī (peace be upon him) used to say, 'There will be tribulation (balāʾ) until the seventy,' and he said, 'After the tribulation, there will be relief.' The seventy have passed, and we have not seen any relief."

Then, Abū Jaʿfar (peace be upon him) replied, "O Thabit! Allah had timed this matter for the seventy, but when Husayn (peace be upon him) was killed, Allah's anger towards the people of the earth intensified, so He delayed it to one hundred and forty years. We told you this, but you disclosed the matter and revealed the secret, so Allah delayed it and did not set a time for it after that with us. **"Allah erases what He wills and establishes what He wills, and with Him is the Mother of the Book."** Abū Ḥamza said, "I mentioned this to Imam Jaʿfar al-Ṣādiq (peace be upon him), and he said, 'That was indeed the case.'"[2]

There is also a narration from Dāwūd al-Raqqī who said, "I said to Abū al-Ḥassan al-Riḍā (peace be upon him), 'May I be your ransom! By Allah, nothing enters my heart concerning your matter except a hadith I heard from Dharīḥ, narrating from Abū Jaʿfar (peace be upon him).' He said, 'And what is it?' I said, 'I heard him say, "Our seventh is our Qāʾim, Allah willing."' He said, 'You are truthful, and Dharīh is truthful, and Abū Jaʿfar (peace be upon him) is truthful.'" Dāwūd said, "By Allah, my doubt further increased. Then he said to me, 'O Dāwūd b. Abī Kalda! By Allah, if the Prophet Moses (peace be upon him) had

---

1. In Shia Islam, Qāʾim Āl Muḥammad (lit. 'the one who shall rise from the family of Muhammad') is an epithet for the Mahdi, the eschatological figure in Islam who is widely believed to restore the religion and justice in the end of time.

2. *Biḥār al-Anwār,* vol. 4, p. 114.

not said to the learned man, **"You will find me, Allah willing, patient,"**[1] he would not have asked him about anything. Similarly, if Abū Jaʿfar (peace be upon him) had not said, "Allah willing," it would have been as he said.' So, I left with increased certainty."[2]

In that context, the revolutionaries started spreading the word, and the matter reached the authorities to the point that it became widespread. Consequently, a group of revolutionaries was arrested, and the Imam was imprisoned and subsequently killed.[3]

The notion of the seventh Imam's uprising became so widespread that the authority used it as a propaganda tool against the revolutionary movement. After poisoning and killing the Imam in the dungeons of Baghdad, they declared: "This is Mūsā b. Jaʿfar, whom the Rawāfiḍ claim will not die. Look at him now."[4]

In reality, the (failure of the revolution) or its delay, and the martyrdom of the Imam who the people expected to lead it, caused a severe shock to some members of the revolutionary movement. It was a difficult test, but later it became evident that this was a wise move as the political situation eventually turned in their favor without the shedding of blood.

Some individuals with personal ambitions for leadership or wealth exploited this shock among the naive people, claiming that Mūsā b. Jaʿfar (peace be upon him) did not die and that he would not die until he fulfilled his mission.

Imam ʿAlī b. Mūsā al-Riḍā (peace be upon him) opposed this corrupt belief until it diminished and had no significant presence. For example, Jaʿfar b. Muḥammad al-Nawfali reported: "I came to al-Riḍā (peace be upon him) while he was at the Qantara of Ibrīq[5]. I greeted

---

1. Quran, Sūrah al-Kahf: 69.
2. *Biḥār al-Anwār,* vol. 48, p. 260.
3. Ibid., p. 291.
4. *Maqātil al-Ṭālibiyīn,* p.505.
5. It is a place in Rāmhurmuz district of Iran's Khuzistān province.

him, sat down, and said, 'May I be your ransom! Some people claim that your father (peace be upon him) is alive.' He replied, 'They lie, may Allah curse them. If he were alive, his inheritance would not have been divided, nor would his women have been married off. By Allah, he has tasted death just as ʿAlī b. Abi Talib (peace be upon him) did.'"[1]

Thus, the confrontation between the Abbasid authority and the revolutionary movement reached its peak, and the comprehensive revolution plan was ready if the secret had not been disclosed and Imam Mūsā al-Kāẓim (peace be upon him) had not been arrested preemptively. There are texts and historical evidences in this regard, which will be mentioned as follows:

The Era of Hārūn al-Rashīd: The Peak of Abbasid Terrorism:

Due to the rising efforts and increasing tendency towards the Ahl al-Bayt (peace be upon them) as well as the increasing likelihood of the Abbasid regime's downfall, Hārūn al-Rashīd exercised unprecedented terrorism in the history of the confrontation between the Abbasid authority and the Imams of the Ahl al-Bayt (peace be upon them).

The practice of Taqiyya – which means dissimulation and working in secrecy – was at its peak during the time of Imam Mūsā (peace be upon him). Perhaps the title "al-Kāẓim" (the one who suppresses his anger) refers to the method of his life, which was marked by Taqiyya and suppressing the anger over the pains and pressures he endured. His other titles also reflect the nature of his era; his followers referred to him as "The Righteous Servant," (ʿAbd al-Ṣāliḥ) "The Pure Soul," (al-Nafs al-Zakiyya) and "The Patient One" (al-Ṣābir). The diversity of his titles indicates the secrecy that characterized the movement in

---

1. *Biḥār al-Anwār,* vol. 4, p. 260.

his era. He was also known as "Abū al-Ḥassan," "Abū ʿAlī," "Abū Ibrāhīm," and "Abū Ismāʿīl."

Our noble Imam, Imam Mūsā Al-Kāẓim (peace be upon him) spent a long period in the Abbasid prisons, and his martyrdom occurred in a tragic manner comparable only to the martyrdom of his grandfather, Abū ʿAbdullah al-Ḥusayn (peace be upon him). This indicates that their fear was immense regarding his potential uprising against their oppression and terrorism, as none of the tyrants wanted to repeat the mistake of Yazīd b. Muʿāwiya, who openly killed the Master of Martyrs (peace be upon him). Instead, they preferred to assassinate the Imams of the Ahl al-Bayt (peace be upon them) to get rid of them and avoid being held accountable by the Muslim masses, who held loyalty and respect for the Ahl al-Bayt (peace be upon them).

Even Hārūn al-Rashīd, in whose prison Imam Al-Kāẓim (peace be upon him) was martyred, tried to deny responsibility for his death, pretending he died naturally, or that his police commander, al-Sindī b. Shāhak, acted without his orders. From this, we understand that the authorities did not risk killing Imam Al-Kāẓim (peace be upon him) unless they felt threatened. However, the Abbasid authority had executed many leaders of the Alawi house in the same manner.

The Ordeal of the Alawi House:

The ordeal of the ʿAlawī house was tremendous during that period. They refused to submit to the regime's terrorism, leading to their imprisonment in dreadful conditions and subjected to all forms of torture. Many of them were also killed. This indicates the strength and threat of the opposition to the regime and highlights the endurance of this pure house in facing calamities for the sake of Allah's messages. It was not, understandably, without reason that the Prophet (peace be upon him and his family) emphasized caring for his family, considering them his heirs, and making them the center of truth. They were likened to Noah's Ark – whoever boarded it was saved, and whoever stayed behind was doomed.

The following story illustrates some of the significant ordeals faced by the Prophet's family from the descendants of Fāṭima and ʿAlī (peace be upon them):

The Story of ʿUbaidullah al-Bazzāz al-Nīshābūrī

ʿUbaidullah al-Bazzāz al-Nīshābūrī, who was an elderly man, narrated:

There was a transaction between me and Ḥumayd b. Qaḥṭaba al-Ṭāʾī al-Ṭūsī, so I traveled to him one day. When he learned of my arrival, he summoned me immediately. I had arrived in my travel clothes, which I had not changed, and it was during the noon prayer in the month of Ramadan.

When I entered, I found him in a room with running water. I greeted him and sat down. A basin and pitcher were brought, and he washed his hands, then ordered me to wash mine. The table-cloth was spread, and I forgot that I was fasting and that it was Ramaḍān. Then I remembered and refrained from eating.

Ḥumayd asked me, "Why don't you eat?" I said, "O Emir, it is Ramaḍān, and I am not ill or have any excuse to break my fast. Perhaps the Emir has an excuse or an illness because of which he is breaking the fast." He replied, "I am not ill and am in good health." Then he wept.

After finishing his meal, I asked, "Why do you weep, O Emir?" He said:

"Hārūn al-Rashīd summoned me one night while he was in Ṭūs. When I entered, I saw a lit candle, a drawn sword, and a servant standing before him. When I stood before him, he looked up at me and asked, 'How loyal are you to the Commander of the Faithful?' I replied, 'With my life and wealth.' He lowered his head and then dismissed me.

I had not been home long when the messenger returned and said, 'The Commander of the Faithful wants to see you again.' I thought to myself, 'By Allah, he must have decided to kill me but hesitated earlier.' So, I returned to him. He looked up at me and asked again, 'How loyal are you to the Commander of the Faithful?' I replied, 'With my life, wealth, family, and children.' He smiled and dismissed me again.

I had just reached home when the messenger came again, saying, 'The Commander of the Faithful has summoned you again.' I presented myself before him once more. He asked, 'How loyal are you to the Commander of the Faithful?' I replied, 'With my life, wealth, family, children, and faith.' He laughed and handed me a sword, saying, 'Take this sword and follow this servant's orders.'

The servant led me to a house with a locked door. He opened it, revealing a well in the middle and three locked rooms. He opened one room, and inside were twenty people with long hair and beards, chained, including old men, middle-aged, and young men. The servant said, 'The Commander of the Faithful orders you to kill them.' They were all Alawi's from the descendants of ʿAlī and Fāṭima (peace be upon them). He began to bring them out one by one, and I beheaded them and threw their bodies and heads into the well until none were left.

Then he opened another room, and there were twenty more Alawi's, descendants of ʿAlī and Fāṭima (peace be upon them), chained. He said, 'The Commander of the Faithful orders you to kill these as well.' He brought them out one by one, and I beheaded them and threw them into the well until none were left.

Finally, he opened the third room, and there were twenty more Alawis, chained, with long hair and beards. He said, 'The Commander of the Faithful orders you to kill these as well.' He brought them out one by one, and I beheaded them and threw them into the well until nineteen were dead. One elderly man remained, who looked at me and said, 'Woe unto you, accursed one! What excuse will you have on the Day of Judgment when you meet our grandfather, the Messenger of Allah (peace be upon him and his family), having killed sixty of his descendants, all born of ʿAlī and Fāṭima (peace be upon them)?' My hand trembled, and I felt terrified. The servant, angry, rebuked me, and I killed the old man too, throwing him into the well.

With this act of killing sixty descendants of the Prophet (peace be upon him and his family), what is the use of my fasting and prayers when I am certain I will be in hell forever?"[1]

The Difficult Circumstances Facing Scholars

The ordeal of the prominent scholars who were loyal to the Ahl al-Bayt (peace be upon them) was also significant. Were they not Shīʿa of the family of Muḥammad? For this reason, they too had to consider the Imams as their role models in facing calamities and difficulties.

One of these scholars who endured the most severe tribulations was Muḥammad b. Abū ʿUmayr al-Azdī, who was considered a highly esteemed scholar. Among the general and the elite, he was regarded as the most reliable, pious, and devout. He was one of the most trustworthy individuals among both the general populace and the elite, the most devout in asceticism, the most pious, and the most devout in worship. It is narrated from Al-Jaḥiẓ that he said: He was unparalleled in his time in all aspects. He also said: Muḥammad b. Abū ʿUmayr al-Azdī was a prominent figure among the "Rafidha" (a derogatory term for Shīʿa). He was imprisoned during the days of Hārūn to force him to take up the position of a judge. It is also said that the reason for his imprisonment was his refusal to disclose the identities of the Shīʿa and supporters of Imam Mūsā b. Jaʿfar, peace be upon him.

Because of this, he was beaten so severely that he was close to confessing due to the intense pain he endured. When Muḥammad b. Yunus b. Abdur Rahman became aware of his intention, he told him: "Fear Allah, O Muḥammad b. Abū Umayr!" Muḥammad demonstrated patience and resilience until Allah facilitated his release.

---

1. *Biḥār al-Anwār,* vol. 48, p. 176 -178.

Al-Kashī narrated that he was beaten with 120 rods during the days of Hārūn, and Sindī b. Shāhak carried out the beating because of Muḥammad b. Abū Umayr's adherence to Shīʿa Islam. He was imprisoned and not released until he paid 21,000 dirhams from his own money.

It is also narrated that Maʾmūn imprisoned him until he appointed him as a judge in some regions. Shaykh Mufid has narrated in *al-Ikhtiṣāṣ* as such: He was imprisoned for seventeen years. During his imprisonment, his sister buried his books, which remained buried for four years, leading to their destruction. It is said that the books were left in a room and were ruined by rain, so he narrated from his memory and from what he had previously conveyed to people. He experienced the time of Imam Al-Kāẓim (peace be upon him) but did not narrate from him, and he narrated from Imam al-Riḍā and Imam Jawād, peace be upon them. He died in the year 217 AH.[1]

Infiltrating the Abbasid Government

Perhaps one of the clearest indications of the strength of the scholarly movement during the time of Imam Al-Kāẓim (a) was the expansion of its influence within the government and some of its official institutions. It is likely that the head of the regime was aware, albeit in a general sense, of the loyalty of his men to the Ahl al-Bayt (peace be upon them), but he felt incapable of overthrowing them due to various reasons and factors.

Before recounting some historical stories of this infiltration, it is worth knowing that the robustness of the organizational network from which the scholarly movement benefited and which allowed its members to be placed at different levels and in various sensitive institutions of the regime can be considered, can be considered a model for what organizational and scholarly groups everywhere

1. *Biḥār al-Anwār,* vol. 4, p. 179; Margin, from *Sharḥ Mashīkhat al-Faqīh,* p. 56-57.

should be like everywhere.

1. It seems that some provincial governors, or as they were called at that time *wālī's*, were affiliated with the movement. For example, the city of Ray, which is present-day Tehran, was one of the major centers at that time, yet its governor was one of the supporters and enthusiasts of the Ahl al-Bayt, peace be upon them. This point can be inferred from the book "Qaḍāʾ Ḥuqūq al-Muʾminīn" written by Abū ʿAlī b. Tahir al-Ṣūrī, based on the narration from a man from Ray: One of the secretaries of Yaḥyā b. Khālid was appointed as governor over us. I owed him some remaining taxes, which, if demanded, would have made me poor. I feared that he would force me to pay the taxes and deprive me of the comfort I was in. I was told that he (the governor) followed this (Shīʿa) sect, but I was afraid to approach him because if this news was false, I would fall into the situation I feared. The situation continued until I sought refuge in Allah and went to visit the House of Allah and visited my master, Imam Mūsā b. Jaʿfar (a), and complained about my situation to him. After listening to my grievances, the Imam wrote a letter saying:

"In the name of Allah, the Most Compassionate, the Most Merciful. Know that Allah has a shadow under His throne where none resides except those who do good to their brother, relieve his distress, or bring joy to his heart. This is your brother. Peace be upon you."

After performing Hajj, I returned to my city and went to the governor at night, seeking permission to see him. I said, "I am the messenger of Imam Mūsā b. Jaʿfar (peace be upon him)." Yaḥyā himself came barefoot, opened the door for me, kissed me, embraced me, and kissed my forehead. Every time he asked me about seeing the Imam, he repeated these actions. When I informed him of the Imam's well-being, he rejoiced and thanked Allah. Then he took me into his house, seated me in the highest part of the room, and sat opposite me. I presented him with the letter, which he kissed standing and read. Then he called for money and clothes. He divided the money dinar by dinar, dirham by dirham, and the clothes item by item with me. He even paid me the value of items that could not be divided. Whatever he gave me, he asked, "Brother, have I made you happy?" I replied, "Yes, by Allah, you have increased my happiness." Then he removed my name from the list of tax debtors and gave me a written exemption from paying it.

I bade him farewell and left. I thought to myself that I was unable to repay this man's kindness except by praying for him during my next Hajj and informing Imam Mūsā b. Jaʿfar (peace be upon him) of what he had done. So, I did that. When I saw my master, Imam al-Kāẓim - the seventh Imam (peace be upon him), I narrated to him what had transpired between me and that man. The Imam's face beamed with joy. I said, "My master, did this news make you happy?" He replied, "Yes, by Allah, this news made me happy, and it pleased the Commander of the Faithful, and my grandfather, the Messenger of Allah (peace be upon him and his family), and Allah Almighty."[1]

2. ʿAlī b. Yaqṭīn was a minister to the caliph, overseeing vast lands, and was one of the closest advisors to Hārūn al-Rashīd. Simultaneously, he was a supporter of the Ahl al-Bayt (peace be upon them).[2] We will mention, Allah willing, some hadiths that illustrate the positions of ʿAlī b. Yaqṭīn, revealing that the policy of *taqiyya* (dissimulation) was not a temporary strategy but a long-term working

---

1. *Biḥār al-Anwār*, vol. 48, p. 174.

2. Ali ibn Yaqṭīn ibn Musa, a resident of Baghdad originally from Kufa, was a prominent and well-known figure among his community. He was a client (*mawla*) of the Banu Asad tribe and was known by the nickname Abū al-Hasan. Imam Musa al-Kāẓim (peace be upon him) guaranteed him paradise and ensured that the fire of hell would not burn him. The book *"Rijāl al-Kashī"* contains hadiths that indicate his high status and great significance. Ali ibn Yaqṭīn would bring substantial amounts of wealth to Imam Musa al-Kāẓim, sometimes ranging from one hundred to three hundred thousand. Every year, he would send people to perform Hajj on his behalf. In one year, according to the records, 150 or 300 people performed Hajj in his stead. He would give some of these individuals, such as Kāhlīlī and Abdul Raḥmān ibn al-Ḥajjāj, ten thousand dirhams each, and others twenty thousand dirhams, with the minimum amount paid for this purpose being one thousand dirhams. He also authored books that were narrated by his son Hasan and Ahmad ibn Hilāl. In the year 182 AH, while Imam Musa al-Kāẓim was imprisoned by Hārūn in Baghdad, Ali ibn Yaqṭīn passed away.

strategy. Perhaps the Imams of guidance saw that empowering their men in positions of authority, in one way or another, was the best means of reforming the affairs of the nation. They did not see a need for a rapid change at the top of the power hierarchy, nor did they seek to directly assume the responsibilities of governance, even though the cultural maturity of the nation might not yet have reached the level required for an ideal divine system as envisioned by the Ahl al-Bayt, peace be upon them.

In other words, the strategy of "opposition" to the ruling system by infiltrating its centers and sensitive institutions, thereby depriving the system of its power from within, might have been the best strategy under those circumstances.

A) The Story of the "Robe"

At a time when ʿAlī b. Yaqṭīn was close to Hārūn al-Rashīd, spies constantly surrounded him and other ministers, as Hārūn was tormented day and night by the thought of his ministers being loyal to the rightful Imam, Mūsā b. Jaʿfar (peace be upon him). However, the divine knowledge possessed by the Imams of the Ahl al-Bayt (peace be upon them) prevented Hārūn from proving anything against ʿAlī b. Yaqṭīn. Additionally, ʿAlī b. Yaqṭīn's discipline and strict adherence to orders denied Hārūn many opportunities. One such opportunity was the incident of the "robe," which we will explain below:

Ibrāhīm b. al-Ḥassan b. Rashīd narrated from Ibn Yaqṭīn: "I was standing with Hārūn al-Rashīd when gifts from the king of Rome arrived, among which was a black silk cloak woven with gold, the likes of which I had never seen before. Hārūn noticed me looking at it, so he gifted it to me. I sent it to my master Abū Ibrāhīm (Imam Mūsā Al-Kāẓim, peace be upon him). Nine months passed after this incident.

One day, after having lunch with Hārūn, I returned home. As I entered my house, my attendant, who was holding my robe with a package in his hand, presented a letter to me that was still sealed. He said: 'A man just now gave this to me and told me to give it to you as soon as you arrived.' I broke the seal and saw that the letter was from my master, Imam Mūsā Al-Kāẓim (peace be upon him). The letter stated: 'O ʿAlī, this is the time you need the robe, so I have sent it back to you.' I uncovered the corner of the package and saw the same robe and recognized it.

At that moment, Hārūn's servant entered without permission and said: 'The Commander of the Faithful has summoned you.' I asked: 'What has happened?' He replied: 'I do not know.'

I rode to Hārūn and entered to find him standing with Umar b. Bazi. Hārūn asked, 'What have you done with the robe I gave you?' I said, 'The Commander of the Faithful's gifts to me are many, from robes to other items. Which one are you asking about?' Hārūn said: 'The black silk Roman robe woven with gold.' I said: 'I have not done anything with it except that I wear it occasionally and pray a few rakʿahs in it. Just a short while ago, I had called for it to wear.' Hārūn looked at Umar b. Bazee and said: 'Tell him to bring it.' I sent my servant to bring the robe. When Hārūn saw it, he said to Umar: 'It is not appropriate to speak against ʿAlī b. Yaqṭīn after this.' He then ordered that fifty thousand dirhams be given to me. I took the money and the robe to my house. ʿAlī b. Yaqṭīn continued narrating: 'The person who spoke ill of me to Hārūn was my cousin, but Allah darkened his face and proved him a liar. Thanks are due to Allah.'"

B) Secret Communications

How did the communications between the Imam and his hidden followers like ʿAlī b. Yaqṭīn take place? We do not have extensive details on the nature of these communications. However, a researcher can infer from some scattered reports. For example, an agricultural expert can determine the soil, water, air, seed, and fertilizer quality from a single apple. Similarly, a historian can uncover more details by contemplating the dimensions of a reported historical event. The second incident reveals the nature of the secret communications between the Imams of guidance and their followers:

Muḥammad b. Mas'ud, from al-Ḥusayn b. Ishkīb, from Bakr b. Ṣāliḥ, from Ismā'īl b. ʿAbad al-Qaṣrī, from Ismā'īl b. Salām, and someone else from the Ḥamid family, said: "ʿAlī b. Yaqṭīn sent for us and said, 'Buy two camels and avoid the main road.' He gave us money and letters, instructing us to deliver them to Abū al-Ḥassan Mūsā (peace be upon him) without anyone knowing about us. We went to Kufa, bought two camels, and prepared provisions. We avoided the main road, and when we reached Baṭn al-Rumma, we tied our camels and started eating. As we were doing so, we saw a rider approaching with a servant. As the rider drew near, we recognized him as Abū al-Ḥassan Mūsā (peace be upon him). We stood up, greeted him, and handed him the letters and money we had. He took letters from his sleeve and handed them to us, saying: 'These are the replies to your letters.' We said: 'Our provisions are depleted. If you permit, we would like to enter Medina to visit the grave of the Messenger of Allah (peace be upon him and his family) and replenish our supplies.' He said, 'Give me your provisions.' We handed them to him, and he inspected them with his hand, saying, 'These will be enough to get you to Kufa. As for the grave of Messenger of Allah (peace be upon him and his family), you have seen him. I prayed the Fajr with him and intend to pray Ḍuhr with him. Get back in Allah's protection.'"[1]

C) Taqiyya Even in Wuḍū

Attempts by informants and the regime's investigators to uncover the true nature of ʿAlī b. Yaqṭīn failed, prompting Hārūn himself to spy on him, which also ended in failure, as the following report indicates:

1. *Biḥār al-Anwār,* vol.48, p. 35. It appears that the Imam, peace be upon him, dissuaded them from visiting the grave of the Holy Prophet, peace be upon him, telling them to suffice with seeing his successor directly. This is indicated by his words when he said "As for the grave of Messenger of Allah (peace be upon him and his family), you have seen him."

Muḥammad b. Ismāʿīl narrated from Muḥammad b. al-Faḍl: "There was a disagreement among our companions regarding the wiping of the feet in wuḍū: is it from the toes to the ankles or from the ankles to the toes? ʿAlī b. Yaqṭīn wrote to Abū al-Ḥassan Mūsā (peace be upon him) about it, asking him to write in his own hand what he should follow. Abū al-Ḥassan wrote to him: 'I understand the difference you mentioned in wuḍū. What I instruct you to do is to rinse your mouth three times, sniff water into your nose three times, wash your face three times, comb your beard, wipe your entire head, wipe the outside and inside of your ears, and wash your feet up to the ankles three times. Do not deviate from this.' When the letter reached ʿAlī b. Yaqṭīn, he was astonished by its contents, which contradicted the consensus of the group. Yet, he said, 'My master knows best what he has said, and I will follow his order.' He performed his wuḍū in this manner, contrary to the practices of all the Shīʿa, in compliance with Abū al-Ḥassan's command.

ʿAlī b. Yaqṭīn was accused of being a Rāfiḍī (Shīʿa) who opposed Hārūn al-Rashīd. Hārūn said to one of his close associates: 'There have been many accusations against ʿAlī b. Yaqṭīn of opposing us and inclining towards the Rāfiḍa. I have not seen any shortcomings in his service to me, and I have tested him many times without finding any evidence to support these accusations. I want to investigate him in a way that he will not be aware of so that he cannot protect himself.'

It was said to Hārūn al-Rashīd: 'The Rāfiḍah (a term used to refer to Shīʿa Muslims) – O Commander of the Faithful – differ from the majority in their method of ablution; they do not wash their feet as the Sunni community believes they should. Test him, O Commander of the Faithful, in a way that he will not know, by observing his ablution.' Hārūn al-Rashīd said: 'Indeed, this method will reveal his true state.'

Then, he left him for a while and occupied him with some work in the house until it was time for prayer. ʿAlī b. Yaqṭīn had a private room in the house where he performed his ablution and prayed. When the time for prayer came, Hārūn al-Rashīd stood behind the wall of the room where he could see ʿAlī b. Yaqṭīn but ʿAlī could not see him.

ʿAlī b. Yaqṭīn called for water for ablution, rinsed his mouth three times, inhaled water into his nose three times, washed his face three times, ran his fingers through his beard, washed his hands up to the elbows three times, wiped his head and ears, and washed his feet while Hārūn al-Rashīd watched him.

When Hārūn saw him do this, he could not contain himself and approached him so that ʿAlī could see him. He then called out: "ʿAlī b. Yaqṭīn, whoever claims you are among the Rāfiḍah has lied." Hārūn al-Rashīd's opinion of him improved, and he received a letter from Abū al-Ḥassan (peace be upon him):

"From now on, O ʿAlī b. Yaqṭīn, perform your ablution as Allah has commanded. Wash your face once as an obligation and again for thoroughness (completion), wash your hands up to the elbows in the same manner, wipe the front of your head and the surface of your feet with the remaining moisture from your ablution. What was feared for you has now been removed. Wassalām."[1]

3 - Musayyib was the deputy chief of the police under Sindī b. Shāhak, who was tasked with guarding the Imam. Musayyib was loyal to the Imam, as indicated by some historical accounts. He communicated with the Shīʿa and followed the Imam's instructions. In reality, many who were imprisoned alongside the Imam came to believe in his authority due to witnessing his miracles. For example, Bashshār, a servant of Sindī b. Shāhak, said:

"I was one of the people who harbored the most hatred for the family of Abū Talib. One day, Sindī b. Shāhak summoned me and said: 'Bashshār, I want to entrust you with a task that Hārūn has entrusted to me with confidence.' I said: 'In that case, I have no choice.' Sindī b. Shāhak said: 'This is Mūsā b. Jaʿfar whom Hārūn has entrusted to me, and I am assigning you to guard him.'

1. *Biḥār al-Anwār,* vol.48, p. 38-39.

Bashshar continued: 'Sindī b. Shāhak had imprisoned Mūsā b. Jaʿfar in a room without his family, and I was appointed to guard him. I placed several locks on the door and whenever I had to go somewhere, I left my wife to guard him and she would not leave until I returned.'

Bashshār continued, 'Allah turned my enmity and hatred for the Imam into love and affection.'

One day, the Imam called me and said: 'Bashshār, go to the Qanṭara prison and summon Hind b. al-Ḥajjāj. Tell him that Abū al-Ḥassan orders you to come to him. If he drives you away and shouts at you, tell him: 'I have conveyed the message and the Imam's command to you. If you wish, do as he instructed; if not, do nothing,' and then leave him and return.

Bashshār continued: 'I set out to obey the Imam's command, placed the locks on the door as they were, and left my wife by the door, instructing her not to move until I returned. I went to the Qantara prison and met Hind b. Ḥajjāj, saying: 'Abū al-Ḥassan has summoned you to come to him.' Hind shouted at me and drove me away. I said to him: 'I have conveyed the message to you. If you wish, do as he instructed; if not, do nothing,' and then I left him and returned to Abū al-Ḥassan. My wife was still sitting by the door, and the locks were as they were. I opened each lock until I reached the Imam's room. I saw the Imam and narrated the incident. Imam al-Kāẓim (peace be upon him) said: 'Yes, he came to me and left!'

I returned to my wife and asked: 'Did anyone come and enter this room after I left?' She replied: 'By Allah, no. I did not move from this spot, and the locks remained untouched until you returned!'"[1]

---

1. *Biḥār al-Anwār,* vol.48, p. 241.

Chapter Three

The Miracles and Knowledge of Imam al-Kāẓim (a)

The Miracles of Imam al-Kāẓim:

The miracles of the Imam differ significantly from the notion of extremism (*ghulū*), which is vehemently rejected by Muslims, and the belief in the miracles of the saints (awliya Allah) and the acceptance of their prayers by Allah. The concept of *ghulū* elevates an individual to the level of divinity, suggesting that Allah dwells within his servants and that the servant, in turn, takes the place of Allah, controlling fate himself.

However, belief in the miracles of the noble servants of Allah reflects pure monotheism (tawḥīd) because it rejects any intrinsic transformation in the nature of the Prophet, Imam, or *walī*. These miracles signify that Allah has bestowed His devoted servants with superior knowledge or power.

The Quranic verses emphasize Allah's transcendence and deny any possibility of His dwelling within anything or anyone, condemning polytheistic beliefs. They also remind us of the miracles of the prophets, which are a mark of their honor in Allah's sight, as these miracles occur by Allah's will.

For example, Allah says about Jesus, son of Mary (peace be upon him):

"And a messenger to the Children of Israel, [who will say], 'Indeed I have come to you with a sign from your Lord in that I design for you from clay [that which is] like the form of a bird, then I breathe into it and it becomes a bird by permission of Allah. And I cure the blind and the leper, and I give life to the dead - by permission of Allah. And I inform you of what you eat and what you store in your houses. Indeed, in that is a sign for you, if you

are believers."[1]

The repeated phrase **"by the permission of Allah"** indicates that these miracles do not imply a divine embodiment in the person of Jesus, making him the son of Allah, as the polytheists claim. Instead, it shows that Allah grants His servant whatever He wills, however He wills, and whenever He wills. Similarly, Muslims believe in the Imams and *awliyā'* being honored by Allah with knowledge and ability, which is an integral part of the doctrine of monotheism. Can Allah not assist His obedient servant by granting him knowledge of the unseen? If a servant is sincerely devoted to Allah, why wouldn't Allah bestow this honor upon him? Does Allah not love the repentant, the purified, and those who rely on Him? Does He not love those who obey, worship, and do good, and does He not honor the pious and praise the steadfast, as we read in many chapters of the Quran?

Those who deny the divine support for Allah's righteous servants, especially the infallible Imams, and doubt their miracles, are indeed rejecting the spirit and essence of the Quran and its greatest teachings. The core message of divine teachings is the belief that Allah possesses ultimate power and accomplishes whatever He wills, with His actions based solely on profound wisdom. This wisdom manifests in rewarding the righteous and punishing the wicked.

If wrongdoers and do-gooders were equal before Allah, and He did not support the believers or humiliate the disbelievers and hypocrites, what benefit would there be in believing in His power and wisdom?

Imam Mūsā b. Ja'far (peace be upon him) exemplified this. He was closely associated with the Quran and was the most devout servant of Allah and the greatest adherent to His commands in his time. He performed miracles and possessed honors acknowledged by all Muslims. However, given the scope of this book, we will only mention a few of these miracles here:[2]

---

1. Quran 3:49

2. Al-'Allāma Muḥammad Bāqir al-Majlisī has dedicated a major portion of the 48th

1. Allah saved His righteous servant, Mūsā b. Ja῾far, peace be upon him, from the tyrants of his time because of his reliance on and devotion to Him. Similarly, Allah saves the believers.

It is narrated by ῾Ubaydullah b. Ṣāliḥ, who said: The gatekeeper of Al-Faḍl b. al-Rabī῾ told me that Al-Faḍl b. Al-Rabī῾ said: One night, I was in bed with one of my maidservants. In the middle of the night, I heard the door move. I became fearful. The maidservant said it might be the wind. Shortly thereafter, I saw the door to the room we were sleeping in open, and suddenly 'Masrur Kabir' entered without greeting me and said, "The Commander of the Faithful has summoned you."

I lost hope for my life, thinking that Masrur entering without permission and without greeting could only mean death. I was in a state of impurity, so I did not dare ask him to allow me to bathe. The maidservant, seeing my confusion and panic, said, "Trust in Allah and get up." I got up, dressed, and went out with him until I reached the house of the Caliph. I greeted the Commander of the Faithful, who was in his bed, and he returned the greeting. I fell to the ground. He asked, "Are you frightened?" I replied, "Yes, O Commander of the Faithful." He let me be alone for a while until I calmed down, then he said to me: "Go to our prison and bring Mūsā b. Ja῾far to me, give him thirty thousand dirhams, dress him in five garments, mount him on three mounts, and give him the choice to stay with us or leave for any place he wishes."

I asked, "O Commander of the Faithful, do you order me to release Mūsā b. Ja῾far?" He replied, "Yes." I asked three more times, and he replied, "Yes. Woe unto you! Do you want me to break my oath?" I asked, "What oath, O Commander of the Faithful?" He replied, "I was lying in bed when suddenly a dark-complexioned man, taller than anyone I had seen, appeared, sat on my chest, and placed his hand on

---

volume of his *Biḥār al-Anwār* to some of the miracles of Imam Mūsā al-Kāẓim, peace be upon him. See pages 29 to 100.

my throat. He said, 'Have you imprisoned Mūsā b. Ja'far unjustly?' I replied, 'I will release him and give him robes and gifts.' He then made me swear an oath to this effect and got up from my chest, nearly causing my soul to depart."

Faḍl continued, "I left Hārūn and went to visit Imam Mūsā b. Ja'far in prison. I saw him standing in prayer. I sat until he finished his prayer. I conveyed the greeting of the Commander of the Faithful and informed him of Hārūn's message. I then gave him the gifts Hārūn had mentioned."

Imam Mūsā b. Ja'far said, "If Hārūn has commanded you to do anything else, do it." I replied, "No, by the right of your grandfather, the Messenger of Allah, he commanded me to do only this." The Imam said, "I have no need for the robes, mounts, or money with others' rights in them." I insisted, "I implore you, do not reject these gifts, for Hārūn will become angry." The Imam replied, "Do as you please," and I took his hand and brought him out of the prison.

Then I asked him: "O son of the Messenger of Allah, tell me the reason for this honor you received from this man, as I have a right to know for the good news I brought to you and for what Allah has granted through me."

He replied: "I saw the Prophet, peace be upon him and his family, in a dream on the night of Wednesday. He said to me, 'O Mūsā, are you imprisoned and wronged?' I replied, 'Yes, O Messenger of Allah, imprisoned and wronged.' He repeated this three times, then said: 'I know not but that it may be a trial for you, and a grant of (worldly) livelihood (to you) for a time.'[1] Observe a fast tomorrow, then follow it with fasting on Thursday and Friday. When it is time to break your fast, pray twelve rak'ahs, reciting al-Fātiḥa and twelve times Sūrah al-Ikhlāṣ in each rak'ah. After completing four rak'ahs, prostrate and say:

يا سابِقَ الْفَوْتِ، يا سامِعَ كُلِّ صَوْتٍ، يا مُحْيِي الْعِظامَ وَهِيَ رَمِيمٌ بَعْدَ الْمَوْتِ،

---

1. Quran, 21: 111.

أَسْأَلُكَ بِإِسْمِكَ الْعَظِيمِ الْأَعْظَمِ أَنْ تُصَلِيَ عَلى مُحَمَّدٍ عَبْدِكَ وَرَسُولِكَ وَعَلى أَهْلِ بَيْتِهِ الطَّيِّبِينَ الطَّاهِرِينَ وَأَنْ تَجْعَلَ لِي الْفَرَجَ مِمَّا أَنا فيهِ.

'O You who precedes all missed opportunities, O You who hears every sound, O You who revives the bones while they are decayed after death, I ask You by Your Great and Most Great Name to bless Muḥammad, Your servant and messenger, and his pure and righteous family, and to hasten my relief from what I am in.' So, I did as you saw. '"[1]

2. Our master Mūsā al-Kāẓim, peace be upon him, prayed to save some believers from his Shīʿa from the oppression of the tyrant, and Allah answered his prayer. History records that Ṣāliḥ b. Waqqād al-Ṭabarī said: I entered upon Mūsā b. Jaʿfar, and he said:

"O Ṣāliḥ! The tyrant - meaning Hārūn - will call you and imprison you in his prison and ask you about me. Tell him that you do not know Mūsā b. Jaʿfar. When you are imprisoned, whoever you want me to release, I will release him by the permission of Allah Almighty."

Ṣāliḥ said: "Hārūn summoned me from Ṭabaristān and asked: "What has Mūsā b. Jaʿfar done? I have heard that he has been with you." I said: "I do not know about Mūsā b. Jaʿfar. O Commander of the Faithful, you are more aware of him and his whereabouts than I am." Hārūn said: "Take him to prison."

By Allah, one night while the other prisoners were asleep, I was standing when suddenly I heard someone say: "O Salih." I replied: "Here I am." He said: "Have you come here?" I said: "Yes, my master." He said: "Rise and follow me." I rose and followed him. When we reached a path, he said: "O Salih! The power is ours, and it is a divine honor that has been granted to us."

I said: "My master, where should I go to be safe from this oppressor?" He said: "Return to your homeland, for he will not reach

1. *Biḥār al-Anwār,* vol. 48, p. 213-215.

you there." Ṣāliḥ said: I returned to Ṭabaristān. By Allah, after that incident, Hārūn never inquired about me again and did not know whether I was still imprisoned or not."[1]

3. Imam al-Kāẓim (a) used to educate his followers on piety and was given divine light to know their secrets. It is narrated by ʿAbdullah b. al-Qāsim b. al-Ḥārith al-Baṭal, from Marazim, who said: "I came to Medina and in the house where I stayed, I saw a beautiful maidservant. I wanted to take pleasure from her, but she refused. When it got dark, I went back to that house and knocked on the door. The same maidservant opened the door. I placed my hand on her chest, she preceded me, and I entered the house. When dawn broke, I went to Imam al-Kāẓim (peace be upon him), and he said: "O Marāzim! He is not our Shia who does not guard himself against his desires in solitude."[2]

4 - He utilized his divine knowledge to educate his followers on discipline, which is essential in all fields of life, especially in jihad. It is reported:

From Muḥammad b. al-Ḥusayn b. ʿAlī, from Hasan al-Wāsiṭī, from Mūsā b. Bakr, who said: "Abū al-Ḥassan the First, peace be upon him, gave me a note containing his needs and said to me:

'Act upon what is in it.' I put it under the prayer mat and neglected it. Later, I found the note in his hand, and he asked me about it. I said: 'It is at home,' he said:

'O Mūsā! When I command you to do something, do it, or I will be angry with you.'"

5 - Sometimes, miracles were required to teach the Shīʿa humility and to keep them away from arrogance and self-importance, so that they would become members of "Allah's Party," which is characterized by unity and equality regardless of wealth, status, or knowledge. Let us read together the story of ʿAlī b. Yaqṭīn, a minister

1. Ibid., p. 66.
2. Ibid., p. 45.

under the tyrants' rule. Due to his position, he may have become arrogant towards other believers. See how the Imam disciplines him and uses his divine power to instill the spirit of piety in him.

From Muḥammad b. ʿAlī al-Ṣūfī, who said: "Ibrāhīm al-Jammāl, may Allah be pleased with him, sought permission to enter upon Abū al-Ḥassan ʿAlī b. Yaqṭīn the minister, but was denied. ʿAlī b. Yaqṭīn performed Hajj that year and sought permission in Medina to meet our master Mūsā b. Jaʿfar, but was denied. The next day, ʿAlī b. Yaqṭīn said: "My master, what is my sin?" He said:

"I denied you because you denied your brother Ibrāhīm al-Jammāl, and Allah has refused to accept your efforts or forgive you unless Ibrāhīm al-Jammāl forgives you." I said: "My master, who can bring me Ibrāhīm al-Jammāl now while I am in Medina and he is in Kufa?"

He said: "When it is night, go to Baqīʿ alone without letting anyone from your companions or servants know, and ride a saddled steed there."

He went to Baqīʿ, rode the steed, and soon found himself at the door of Ibrāhim al-Jammāl in Kufa. He knocked on the door and said: "I am ʿAlī b. Yaqṭīn." Ibrāhīm al-Jamal from inside the house said: "What does ʿAlī b. Yaqṭīn the minister want at my door?" ʿAlī b. Yaqṭīn said: "My matter is serious, and he swore that he would permit him. When he entered, he said: "O Ibrāhīm, my master refuses to accept me or forgive me unless you forgive me." Ibrāhīm said: "May Allah forgive you." ʿAlī b. Yaqṭīn insisted that Ibrāhīm step on his cheek, but he refused. He insisted again, so he did, and ʿAlī b. Yaqṭīn kept saying: "O Allah, bear witness." Then he left, rode the steed, and soon found himself at the door of our master Mūsā b. Jaʿfar, peace be upon him, in Medina. He was permitted to enter and was accepted."[1]

6 - As the leader of the Muslims and the successor of the Messenger of Allah, peace be upon him and his family, who embodied the noble character of Muḥammad, he was compassionate towards the believers

1. Ibid., p. 85.

and distressed by their troubles. Often, he would look with the light of Allah and see the harm that might befall them and hasten to remove or alleviate it in one way or another. Let's read together the following story:

From Ibrāhīm b. Abdul Hamid, who said: "Abū al-Ḥassan wrote me a letter to change my house. I was saddened by this. Ibrahim's house was located in the middle of the mosque and the market. He did not change his house. The messenger informed him again to change his house, but he still did not comply and remained in the same house. The messenger conveyed the same command a third time. Uthman b. Isa said: I was in Medina (and witnessed this event). Ibrahim then moved from that house and took another residence. I was in the mosque. Ibrahim came to the mosque when it was dark. I asked him: 'What happened?' He said: 'Do you not know what happened to me today?' I said: 'No.' He said: 'I went to draw water from the well to perform ablution. When I drew the bucket, it was full of filth, while we used this water to knead our dough. So, we threw away our bread and washed our clothes, which delayed me from coming to the mosque. Now I have rented a house and moved my belongings there. No one remains in the house except a maid, and I am going to bring her now.' I said: 'May Allah bless you.' Then we parted. At dawn, we came out of our houses to go to the mosque. He said: 'Do you know what happened last night?' I said: 'No.' He said: 'By Allah, both floors of my house collapsed and turned upside down.'"[1]

Thus, the Imam provided his advice to his followers on a seemingly minor but important personal matter. In another incident, the Imam advised an individual on a commercial matter that also seemed minor but revealed a significant concern for the affairs of Muslims. The incident is narrated as follows:

"It is narrated from Hasan b. ʿAlī b. Nuʿmān from ʿUthman b. ʿIsā who said: "Imam Mūsā b. Jaʿfar (peace be upon him) entered Medina

---

1. Ibid., p. 45-46.

early one day and saw Ibrāhīm b. ʿAbd al-Ḥamīd heading towards Qubā. He asked him: 'Ibrahim, where are you going?'

He said: 'To Qubā.'

The Imam asked: 'For what purpose?'

He said: 'We buy dates every year. Now I want to go to a man from the Anṣār to buy some dates from him.'

The Imam asked: 'Have you ensured protection from locusts?'

After saying this, the Imam entered Medina, and I went on my way. I told Abū al-ʿIzz about this incident, and he said: 'By Allah, we will not buy dates this year.' Five days had passed when locusts came and destroyed all the dates in the orchard."[1]

The Knowledge of the Imamate

The foundation of prophethood and divine doctrines is built on faith in the unseen, with the most prominent manifestation being the divine knowledge granted to Allah's close servants. Is the book revealed to the Prophet, commanding people to follow him, not from the unseen? How has Allah taught all these great heavenly doctrines and this magnificent book (the Quran), which challenges the world to bring a chapter or even a few verses like it, to His unlettered Prophet?

We read in the book that Jesus, the son of Mary, provided evidence to his people by telling them what they stored in their houses. Thus, the divine knowledge of the Imam, which surpasses the knowledge of people, is evidence that he is supported by Allah, that he is the Imam, and the proof over all people.

How is this knowledge attained? Is it through the inheritance of hadith from the Messenger of Allah through Gabriel from Allah, or through an imprint on the hearts and ears, or through a pillar of light which the Imam looks at whenever Allah wills him to know something, or by the descent of the spirit—which is greater than the

1. Ibid., p. 46, No. 30.

angels—upon him on the Night of Decree (Qadr), revealing matters to him?

The truth is that all these ways and perhaps other means unknown to us can be valid for the Imam to acquire divine knowledge. We need not trouble ourselves to understand the specifics and details of this matter; it is enough to know that the Imam, by Allah's permission, is aware of what is hidden and unknown to people. Through this, Allah bestows favor upon them, and people must obey them.

It has been narrated in a noble hadith from Imam Jaʿfar al-Ṣādiq, peace be upon him:

"I asked him: 'Tell me about the knowledge of your scholar.' He said: 'This knowledge is inherited from the Prophet (peace be upon him and his family) and ʿAlī b. Abi Talib (peace be upon him).' I asked: 'Does this mean that knowledge is cast into your hearts or whispered into your ears?' He said: 'It might be so.'"[1]

Imam al-Kāẓim, relying on this divine knowledge, spoke in all aspects of life. His advice to Hishām, which is a summary of the wisdom of the prophets and a selection of doctrinal viewpoints, is sufficient proof of this claim. What we mention below is a glimpse from the ocean of his abundant knowledge:

1. It is narrated that Isḥāq b. ʿAmmār said: "When Hārūn imprisoned Imam Mūsā (peace be upon him), Abū Yūsuf and Muḥammad b. al-Ḥassan, companions and students of Abū Hanifa, visited the Imam. One of them said to the other: 'We have come to Mūsā b. Jaʿfar for one of two reasons, either to convince him of our views or to argue against him.' They both sat in front of him. Meanwhile, a man appointed by Sindī b. Shāhak to guard the Imam came and said: 'My shift is over, and I am going home. If you need anything, let me know so that I can fulfill it when my shift resumes.' The Imam said: 'I need nothing.' As the man left, the Imam turned to Abū Yūsuf and said: 'How strange is this man! He will die tonight and

1. *Biḥār al-Anwār,* vol. 2, p. 174.

he says he will serve me tomorrow!'

Abū Yūsuf and Muḥammad b. al-Ḥassan left, saying: 'We came to ask him about obligatory and recommended acts, but he now says something as if he has knowledge of the unseen.'

They sent a man to follow the guard and see what happens to him that night. The man waited in a mosque opposite the guard's house. At midnight, cries and wails were heard, and people were seen going to his house. He asked: 'What happened?'

They said: 'So-and-so suddenly died tonight without any illness.'

The man returned to Abū Yūsuf and Muḥammad b. al-Ḥassan and informed them of the incident. They went back to the seventh Imam and said: 'We knew you had knowledge of lawful and unlawful matters, but how did you know this man would die tonight?'

The Imam replied: 'From the door through which the Prophet (peace be upon him and his family) taught his knowledge to ʿAlī b. Abi Talib (peace be upon him).'

Hearing this, they were astonished and could not respond."[1]

Thus, Imam Mūsā b. Jaʿfar (peace be upon him) was granted the knowledge of deaths as was granted before to Allah's prophets and noble saints.

2. Additionally, by Allah's permission, he was aware of various languages spoken by people. In a hadith from Ibn Abi Ḥamza, he said: "I was with Imam Mūsā b. Jaʿfar (peace be upon him) when thirty slaves bought from Abyssinia were brought before him. One of them, who spoke well, conversed with the Imam. Imam Mūsā answered him in the same language. The slave and the entire assembly were amazed, thinking the Imam did not understand their language. The Imam told the slave: 'I will give you money to pay each of these slaves thirty dirhams.' The slaves left, saying: 'He (Imam al-Kāẓim) speaks our language more eloquently than we do, which is a blessing from Allah.

---

1. *Biḥār al-Anwār,* vol. 48, p. 64-65.

ʿAlī b. Abi Ḥamza said: 'I asked the Imam: O son of the Prophet! I saw you speaking to these Abyssinians in their language?!'

The Imam replied: 'Yes.'

I asked: 'Did you only command that slave?' He said: 'Yes, I told him to be kind to the other slaves and give each of them a monthly allowance of thirty dirhams. Because when he spoke, he seemed more knowledgeable than the others; he was from their royal lineage. So, I appointed him over the others to take care of their needs. Besides, he is an honest slave. Then he said: Perhaps you are astonished that I spoke to them in the Abyssinian language.' I said: 'By Allah, yes.'

He said: 'Do not be amazed! What you heard from me is like a bird taking a drop from the sea with its beak. Does the sea lose anything if a bird does so? The Imam is like the sea; what he possesses never ends, and his wonders are more than the wonders of the sea.'"[1]

3. In another narration, ʿAlī b. Abi Ḥamza said: "Abū Al-Ḥassan (peace be upon him) sent me to a man who was selling a plate in front of him for a penny. He said: 'Give him these eighteen dirhams and tell him that Abū al-Ḥassan says: Benefit from these dirhams, for they will suffice you until you die.' When I gave him the money, he cried. I asked him: 'Why are you crying?' He replied: 'Why shouldn't I cry when the time of my death has arrived?' I said: 'What is with Allah is better than what you are in.' He then asked: 'Who are you, O servant of Allah?' I said: 'ʿAlī b. Abi Ḥamza.' He said: 'By Allah, my master told me that he would send me a message with ʿAlī b. Abi Hamza.' ʿAlī said: 'I stayed for about twenty nights, then I came to him and found him sick. I said: 'Advise me on what you want me to carry out from your wealth?' He said: 'When I die, marry my daughter to a righteous man, then sell my house and give its price to Abū al-Ḥassan, and bear witness to my washing, burial, and prayer.' When I buried him, I married his daughter to a believing man, sold his house, and brought its price to Abū Al-Ḥassan (peace be upon him). He approved

---

1. *Biḥār al-Anwār,* vol. 48, p. 70.

it, prayed for mercy for him, and said: 'Return these dirhams and give them to his daughter.'"[1]

4 - Since the knowledge of the Imams comes from Allah, and nothing in the heavens and the earth is beyond Allah's power, His wisdom may dictate granting His knowledge to a child in the cradle, as He did with Jesus, son of Mary, and John, son of Zechariah (peace be upon them). Similarly, He demonstrated His power in the person of Imam al-Kāẓim (peace be upon him), as narrated in a revered hadith by ʿIsā Shalaqān: "I went to Abū ʿAbdullah (Imam Jaʿfar al-Ṣādiq, peace be upon him) wanting to ask him about Abū Al-Khaṭṭāb. Before I could sit down, he said to me: 'O ʿIsā, why have you not met my son to ask him about everything you want?'

ʿIsā said: 'I went to the Righteous Servant (i.e. Imam Mūsā, peace be upon him) while he was sitting in the writer's class with a trace of ink on his lips. He said to me: 'O ʿIsā, Allah has taken the covenant of the Prophets for prophecy, and they never turned away from it, and He has taken the covenant of the successors for succession, and they never turned away from it, and He has granted some people faith for a time and then takes it away from them, and Abū al-Khaṭṭāb is among those to whom faith was granted and then taken away by Allah.' I embraced him and kissed his forehead, then said: 'May my father and mother be your ransom! **Offspring, some of whom are from others, and Allah is Hearing, Knowing.'**[2] Then I returned to Imam Jaʿfar al-Ṣādiq (peace be upon him) who asked me: 'What did you do, O ʿIsā?' I told him: 'May my father and mother be your ransom! I went to him and he told me without me asking all that I wanted to ask him. By Allah, I knew at that moment that he is the master of this matter.' He said: 'O ʿIsā, my son, this one you saw, if you asked him about everything between the covers of the Quran, he would have answered you with knowledge.' Then he took him out of the writer's class that

1. *Biḥār al-Anwār,* vol. 48, p. 76.

2. Quran, Sūrah Āl-e ʿImrān, verse 34.

day."[1]

5 - When the veil between the Lord and His servant falls, and when spiritual purity and divine knowledge reach their peak, the world comes obediently to the righteous servant, as Allah said in the Qudsi Hadith: "My servant, obey Me, and you will be like (or similar to) Me, saying to a thing 'Be' and it will be, and you will say to a thing 'Be' and it will be." This is how Shaqīq al-Balkhī narrates an aspect of the grace that Allah bestowed upon our seventh Imam, Mūsā b. Jaʿfar (peace be upon him). He says: "I embarked on a journey to Mecca to perform Ḥajj in the year 149 AH, and stayed at Al-Qādisiyya. As I watched people in their adornment and abundance, I saw a handsome young man of wheat-colored complexion, weak in appearance. Over his clothes, he wore a woolen cloak and was wrapped in a shawl, with sandals on his feet. He sat alone, so I said to myself: 'This young man is among the Sufi's who want to be a burden on people during their journey. By Allah, I will go to him and reprimand him.' As I approached him, he said: 'O Shaqīq, **'avoid much suspicion, for some suspicion is a sin.''**[2] Then he left me and walked away. I said to myself: 'What a great event! He spoke what was in my mind and mentioned my name. He must be a righteous servant of Allah. I must follow him and asked him to forgive me.' I hurried after him but could not catch up with him, and he disappeared from my sight. When we arrived at Wāqiṣa, I saw him praying with trembling limbs and tears flowing. I said to myself: 'This is my companion; I will go to him and seek his forgiveness.' I waited until he finished praying. Thereupon, I approached him. When he saw me coming, he said: 'O Shaqiq, recite: **'But indeed, I am the Perpetual Forgiver of whoever repents and believes and does righteousness and then continues in guidance.'**[3] Then he left me and walked away. I said: 'This young man is indeed among the Abdal (Allah's noble servants), he spoke of my secret

---

1. *Biḥār al-Anwār,* vol. 4, p. 58.
2. Quran, Sūrah al-Ḥujrāt, verse 12.
3. Quran, Sūrah Ṭahā, verse 82.

twice.'

When we arrived at Zubāla, I saw him standing by a well with a small vessel in his hand, trying to draw water. The vessel fell into the well while I was watching. He looked up at the sky and said: 'You are my Lord when I thirst for water, and my sustenance when I desire food. O Allah, my Lord, I have no other vessel, do not let me be without it.'

Shaqīq said: 'By Allah, I saw the water of the well rise up, and he reached out, took the vessel, filled it with water, performed ablution, and prayed four rakʿahs. Then he turned towards a sand dune, scooped sand with his hand, and placed it in the vessel, stirred it, and drank. I approached him and greeted him, and he returned the greeting. I said: 'Give me some of what Allah has blessed you with.'

He said: 'O Shaqiq, Allah's blessings on us are manifest and hidden, have good thoughts about your Lord.'

Then he handed me the vessel, and I drank from it, finding it to be a mixture of sweetened flour and sugar. By Allah, I have never tasted anything more delicious or fragrant. I was satisfied and no longer desired food or drink for several days. Then I did not see him until we entered Mecca. I saw him one night near the Dome of the Drink (Qubba al-Sharāb), praying with devotion, groaning, and weeping. He continued like that until the night ended. When he saw the dawn, he sat in his prayer place, glorifying Allah, then stood up and prayed the dawn prayer. He circumambulated the Kaʿba seven times and went out. I followed him and saw that he had attendants and followers, contrary to what I saw on the journey. People gathered around him, greeting him. I asked someone close to him: 'Who is this young man?' He said: 'This is Mūsā b. Jaʿfar b. Muḥammad b. ʿAlī b. al-Ḥusayn b. ʿAlī b. Abi Ṭālib (peace be upon them).' I said: 'I am not surprised that such wonders are shown by this noble master.'"

And indeed, some of the early poets have composed verses about Shaqīq's encounter with Imam Mūsā al-Kāẓim, and I will mention some of them here:

Ask Shaqīq al-Balkhī about him and what he witnessed, and what he saw,	سَلْ شَقِيقَ الْبَلْخِيِّ عَنْهُ وَمَا عَايَنَ مِنْهُ وَمَا الَّذِي كَانَ أَبْصَرَ
He said: When I went for Ḥajj, I saw a person pale in color, thin in body, and dark in complexion,	قَالَ: لَمَّا حَجَجْتُ عَايَنْتُ شَخْصا شَاحِبَ اللَّوْنِ نَاحِلَ الْجِسْمِ أَسْمَرَ
Walking alone without provisions, and I kept wondering,	سَائِراً وَحْدَهُ وَلَيْسَ لَهُ زَادٌ فَمَا زِلْتُ دَائِماً أَتَفَكَّرُ
And thought he was asking people, not knowing he was the Greatest Pilgrim,	وَتَوَهَّمْتُ أَنَّهُ يَسْأَلُ النَّاسَ وَلَمْ أَدْرِ أَنَّهُ الْحَجُّ الْأَكْبَرُ
Then I saw him as we descended near Fayd, on the red dune,	ثُمَّ عَايَنْتُهُ وَنَحْنُ نُزُولٌ دُونَ فَيْدٍ عَلَى الْكَثِيبِ الْأَحْمَرِ
Putting sand in the vessel and drinking it, so I called to him, my mind bewildered,	يَضَعُ الرَّمْلَ فِي الْإِنَاءِ وَيَشْرَبُه فَنَادَيْتُهُ وَعَقْلِي مُحَيَّرٌ
Give me a drink, and he handed it to me, and I saw it was sweetened flour and sugar,	سْقِنِي شَرْبَةً فَنَاوَلَنِي مِنْهُ فَعَايَنْتُهُ سَوِيقاً وَسُكَّرْ
So, I asked the pilgrims: Who is this? They said: This is Imam Mūsā b. Jaʿfar. [1]	فَسَأَلْتُ الْحَجِيجَ: مَنْ يَكُ هَذَا؟ قِيلَ: هَذَا الْإِمَامُ مُوسَى بْنُ جَعْفَر.

1. *Biḥār al-Anwār,* vol. 8, p. 80 – 82.

Chapter Four

His Character and Virtues

His Character and Virtues:

Allah made His prophets and the bearers of His messages human so that they could serve as evidence to people and be followed. If they had been angels, people would have said: "What do we have to do with angels? Aren't they of a different nature?" Indeed, humans are naturally inclined towards loving virtue. When it is embodied in a person, their love for it increases, motivating them to follow and strive to be like that person.

If you were to give someone a detailed lecture on the value of benevolence, it would not have as much impact as telling them a story about a benevolent man. The noble characters of the Imams from the Ahl al-Bayt (peace be upon them) serve as the best educational method, and they are truly the highest examples of goodness and virtue. Their lives, filled with noble deeds, provide the strongest evidence for the soundness of their approach to education and their plan for life. Their lives, rich with noble deeds, are the best evidence of the soundness of their educational methods and way of life, and their thoughts, transmitted by narrators, provide a correct and rightful interpretation of the Quran. Were these honorable figures not human? How then did they achieve such greatness? And did they not attain this lofty status by implementing the very ideas narrated from them? Are we not seeking to achieve greatness and excellence ourselves? Therefore, let us read these thoughts and align our actions with them.

The truth is that history has only conveyed a small portion of the conduct of the Imams to us, as they were always surrounded by the propaganda of oppressive governments to the extent that, in some periods, narrating their virtues put the narrator at risk. A poet like

Dabel carried his execution plank on his back for 25 years due to his praise of Ahl al-Bayt (peace be upon them)! Nonetheless, the narrations about their virtues that have reached us constitute a complete and educational compendium of moral excellences.

Since Imam Mūsā al-Kāẓim (peace be upon him) lived during one of the most challenging periods of struggle and the most difficult times of taqiyya (dissimulation) and concealment, the recording of his stories and the breaking through the barriers imposed by the ruling regime to reach future generations is itself considered a miracle. It is incumbent upon us to reason through these stories that have reached us, even though we know that what has come to us is but a drop of the miracles and astonishing tales of that noble personage.

A) His Worship and Asceticism:

One of the most prominent signs of leaders of schools of thought is their asceticism and piety and devotion to Allah. The era in which Imam Mūsā al-Kāẓim (peace be upon him) lived is known as the "Golden Age." At that time, the palaces of Abbasid rulers were filled with enormous wealth and witnessed lavish and expensive celebrations. Some of these scenes can be read in the book *"One Thousand and One Nights."* In such an age, Ibrahim b. Abdul Hamid said:

"I went to the house of Imam Mūsā al-Kāẓim. He was standing in prayer. In his house, there was nothing except a woven mat made of palm leaves (or a very rough garment) and a hanging sword and a Quran."[1]

He (peace be upon him) would walk to the House of Allah (the Kaʿba) out of extreme humility and dedication in worship. Considering the distance between Medina and Mecca, which is about 400 kilometers, and the nature of the desert in the Hijaz, one can

1. *Biḥār al-Anwār,* vol. 48, p. 100.

understand the extent of the Imam's endurance for the sake of Allah.

ʿAlī b. Jaʿfar said: "We went out with my brother Mūsā b. Jaʿfar (peace be upon him) for four Umrahs in which he walked to Mecca with his family and children. In one of them, he walked for twenty-six days, another for twenty-five days, another for twenty-four days, and the last for twenty-one days."[1]

Regarding his great love for prayer, which is the light of the believers' eyes and the hour of meeting between two friends, the following narration states:

"It is narrated that Imam Mūsā b. Jaʿfar (peace be upon him) performed the night prayers and connected them with Morning Prayer. Then he would engage in post-prayer supplications until sunrise, and then he would prostrate until near noon, without raising his head from prostration or ceasing to praise Allah. He would frequently pray and always say:

'O Allah, I ask you for ease at the time of death, and forgiveness at the time of reckoning.'

One of his other prayers was: 'The sin of your servant is great, so let Your pardon be generous.'

He would weep a great deal out of fear of Allah, to the extent that his beard would be soaked with tears. He was more diligent than others in maintaining family ties and taking care of the poor in Medina."[2]

Indeed, the Imam's diligence in worshiping his Lord and devoting himself through prayers and supplications is what elevated him to a praiseworthy station, enabling him to bear the burdens of the message he upheld and sacrificed for its propagation. His prayers were his greatest solace under the oppression of tyrants. Ahmad b. ʿAbdullah narrated from his father:

---

1. Ibid.
2. Ibid., p. 102.

"I entered upon al-Faḍl b. al-Rabīʿ while he was sitting on a roof. He said to me: 'Look over this house and see what you see.' I said: 'A discarded garment.' He said: 'Look carefully.' I said: 'A man prostrating.' He said to me: 'Do you know him? He is Mūsā b. Jaʿfar. I observe him night and day and have never seen him in any state other than this. He prays the dawn prayer, continues with supplication until the sun rises, then he prostrates and remains prostrating until the sun sets. He has appointed someone to inform him of the prayer times. When he is informed, he jumps up to pray without renewing his ablution. This is his regular habit. When he prays the night prayer, he breaks his fast, then renews his ablution, and prostrates, continuing to pray throughout the night until dawn.' Some of his attendants said: 'I often heard him saying in his prayer:

"O Allah, You know that I used to ask You to free me for Your worship. O Allah, You have done so; for You is the praise."'[1]

As for his recitation of the Quran, Hafs tells us: "I have not seen anyone more fearful for himself than Mūsā b. Jaʿfar (peace be upon him), nor more hopeful for the people than him. His recitation was sorrowful, and when he recited, it was as if he were speaking to a person."[2]

The Quran taught him the highest values, including concern for his *nafs* (soul), diligent efforts to purify it, save it from Allah's wrath, and reform it to be a place of the Creator's love and pleasure.

He always hoped for the best for people, and his hope was not devoid of action. He drew closer to Allah by doing good to people. He would seek out the poor among the Ahl al-Bayt and deliver to them at night whatever they needed without them knowing from which direction it came.[3]

---

1. Ibid., p. 107-108.
2. Ibid., p. 111.
3. Ibid., p. 108.

B) His Generosity and Benevolence

With trust and reliance on Allah, the reward for the benevolent increases, with the belief that He is the Provider, the Possessor of Strength. A believer gives generously without fear of poverty. The Imams of guidance are the highest examples of generosity and benevolence. Imam Mūsā b. Jaʿfar (peace be upon him), despite living under harsh conditions, was renowned for this quality far and wide.

A famous historical narration by Muḥammad b. ʿAbdullah al-Bakrī states:

"I came to Medina in search of a loan, but I failed to obtain it. I said to myself: 'If I go to Abū al-Ḥassan (peace be upon him) and complain to him, perhaps he can help.' So, I went to his farm and met him. The Imam came towards me with his servant who was carrying a dish containing some half-cooked meat and nothing else. The Imam began to eat and I also ate. Then he asked me about my need, so I told him my story. He went inside briefly and then came out, handed his servant a pouch, and gave me 300 dinars. Then he left, and I mounted my animal and returned."[1]

It is narrated by Abū al-Faraj al-Iṣfahānī in "*Maqātil al-Ṭālibiyīn*" from Yaḥyā b. al-Ḥassan:

"Mūsā b. Jaʿfar (peace be upon him) would send a pouch of dinars to any man who displeased him. His pouches ranged between 300 to 200 dinars, and they became known as Mūsā's pouches."

A remarkable story in history narrates that Mansur, the Abbasid Caliph, invited Imam Mūsā b. Jaʿfar to attend a New Year's celebration and to receive the gifts and presents from the people. The Imam said: I searched through the reports narrated from my grandfather, the Messenger of Allah (peace be upon him), but I did not find any mention of this celebration. Rather, it is a tradition of the Persians and Islam has abolished it. I seek refuge in Allah from

1. Ibid., p. 102.

reviving something that Islam has erased. Mansur responded: "I do this to win the hearts and loyalty of the army and I ask you by Allah the Great to sit." So, he sat, and the kings, princes, and soldiers entered to congratulate him, bringing gifts. At the end, an elderly man entered and said:

"O son of the daughter of the Messenger of Allah, I am a poor man with no money to offer you. But I present to you three lines of poetry my grandfather said about your grandfather, al-Ḥusayn b. ʿAlī (peace be upon him):

I am amazed at the polished sword that has adorned you,	عَجِبْتُ لِمَصْقُولٍ عَلَاكَ فِرِنْدُهُ
On the day of battle, dust has covered you.	يَوْمَ الْهِيَاجِ وَقَدْ عَلَاكَ غُبَارُ
And at the arrows that have pierced you, while noble women,	وَلِأَسْهُمٍ نَفَذَتْكَ دُونَ حَرَائِرَ
Call upon your grandfather, their tears flowing abundantly.	يَدْعُونَ جَدَّكَ وَالدُّمُوعُ غِزَارُ
Why did the arrows not shrink back and respect,	أَلَّا تَغَضْغَضَتِ السِّهَامُ وَعَاقَهَا
Revere, and honor your body?	عَنْ جِسْمِكَ الْإِجْلَالُ وَالْإِكْبَارُ

The Imam accepted the gift and said: 'Sit down, may Allah bless you.' He raised his head to the servant and said: 'Go to the Commander of the Faithful and inform him of this wealth and what to do with it.' The servant returned and said: 'It is all a gift from me to him; he can do with it as he pleases.' Mūsā (peace be upon him) then said to the old man: 'Take all this money; it is a gift from me to you.'"[1]

With his generosity and nobility, Imam al-Kāẓim (peace be upon him) treated his enemies and opponents kindly, thereby making them his friends. It is narrated that a man from the lineage of the second caliph lived in Medina and whenever he saw Imam Al-Kāẓim (peace

---

1. Ibid., p. 108.

be upon him), he would harass and insult him, even cursing Imam ʿAlī (peace be upon him).

One day, one of Imam al-Kāẓim's companions said, "Allow us to kill this wicked man," but the Imam strongly forbade them from this thought and asked, "Where is that man?" They said, "He is in one of the outskirts of Medina, farming." The Imam set out to see him and found him in his field. He entered the man's field with his horse. The man shouted, "Do not trample our crops," but the Imam ignored him and continued until he reached him. Then he dismounted and, with a cheerful and smiling face, sat beside the man and asked, "How much have you spent on your farming?" The man replied, "One hundred dinars." The Imam asked, "How much do you hope to earn from it?" The man answered, "I do not have knowledge of the unseen." The Imam said, "I asked, how much do you hope to earn?" The man said, "I hope to earn two hundred dinars."

Then Imam al-Kāẓim (peace be upon him) took out a bag containing three hundred dinars and said, "Take this bag of dinars, and your crop is still intact. Allah will grant you what you hope for." The man stood up and kissed the Imam's head and asked for his forgiveness. The Imam smiled and returned. The Imam went to the mosque and saw that the same man was sitting there. When he saw the Imam, he said, "Allah knows best where to place His message." His companions went to him and asked, "What is your story? You used to speak differently about him (Imam al-Kāẓim)!" The man replied: "You heard what I said", and he started praying for the Imam. His companions argued with him, but he continued to pray for the Imam. When the Imam returned home, he asked his companions who wanted to kill the man: "Which is better, what you wanted or what I did? I have rectified his affairs and spared you his harm."[1]

---

1. *Biḥār al-Anwār,* vol. 56, p.102 – 103.

C) His Knowledge

We have previously discussed the knowledge of the Imam (peace be upon him). Here, we continue this discussion by recounting an interesting narration about his knowledge.

It is reported that Muḥammad b. al-Nuʿmān, known as Abū Ḥanīfa, the founder of the Ḥanafī school of thought, said:

"I saw Mūsā b. Jaʿfar when he was a young boy in his father's vestibule. I asked him: 'Where does a stranger among you relieve himself?' He looked at me and said:

'He hides behind a wall, avoids the eyes of neighbors, steers clear of riverbanks, and avoids orchards, courtyards, thoroughfares, and mosques. He does not face the Qibla nor turn his back to it. After that, he can relieve himself wherever he wants.'

Abū Ḥanīfa said, 'When I heard this from him, he became great in my eyes and gained a high status in my heart. Then I asked him another question and said, 'May I be your ransom, who is the source of sin?' The child looked at me and said, 'Sit down so I can tell you.' I sat down, and he said:

'Sin must be either from the servant or from Allah or from both. If it is from Allah, then He is too just and fair to wrong His servant for something he did not do. If it is from both, then Allah is the stronger partner and should not wrong His weaker partner. If it is from the servant alone, then the command and prohibition apply to him, and he alone deserves reward and punishment, and Heaven and Hell are for him.'

I said: 'A lineage, some of which are from others.[1]'"[2]

Al-Khaṭīb al-Baghdādī in *Tārīkh al-Baghdād*, al-Samʿānī in *al-Risālah al-Qawmiyya,* Aḥmad al-Muʾadhdhin in *al-Arbaʿīn*," Abū ʿAbdullah Ibn Baṭṭā in *al-Ibāna*, and al-Thaʿlabī in *Al-Kashf wal-*

---

1. Quran, Sūrah Āl-e ʿImrān verse 34.
2. *Biḥār al-Anwār,* vol. 48, p.104.

Bayān have reported:

"Ahmad b. Ḥanbal, despite his deviation from the Ahl al-Bayt, said: 'Mūsā b. Jaʿfar narrated to me from his father, who narrated from his grandfather, until he reached the Prophet (peace be upon him and his family), and then said: This chain of narration, if read to a madman, would cure him.'"

His Courage and Integrity

Imam Mūsā b. Jaʿfar (peace be upon him) bore the burdens of the prophets' missions with the same great determination of the prophets (peace be upon them). He confronted every tyranny and every accumulation of corruption with absolute confidence in the Lord of the Worlds.

When al-Faḍl b. al-Rabīʿ came to him and said, "Prepare for punishment, O Abū Ibrāhīm, may Allah have mercy on you," he replied, "Isn't the One who owns the world and the Hereafter with me? No harm can befall me today unless Allah wills it."[1]

When he was brought before Hārūn al-Rashīd, the tyrant who once addressed the clouds and boasted about the vastness of his dominion, saying, "Move east or west, wherever you go, your revenue will come to me," Hārūn asked him, "What is this house?"

The Imam replied, "This is the house of the transgressors. Allah Almighty said: **'I will turn away from My signs those who are arrogant upon the earth without right; and if they should see every sign, they will not believe in it. And if they see the way of righteousness, they will not adopt it as a way.'"**[2]

Hārūn then asked, "So whose house is it?" The Imam replied, "The world is a brief period for our followers and a trial for others."

Hārūn asked, "Why does the owner of this house (Allah) not take

---

1. Ibid., p. 215.
2. Qur'an 7:146

it back?" The Imam replied, "It was taken from him while it was thriving (inhabited), and he will not take it back unless it is thriving again."

Hārūn asked, "Where are your followers?" The Imam recited, **"Those who disbelieved among the People of the Scripture and the polytheists were not to be parted until there came to them clear evidence."**[1]

Hārūn then said to him, "So we are disbelievers?" The Imam replied, "No, but as Allah said: 'They exchanged the favor of Allah for disbelief and led their people to the house of destruction.'"[2]

At this, Hārūn became angry and harsh towards him.[3]

From his prison, surrounded by the criminal guards of the authorities, the Imam wrote a letter to Hārūn al-Rashīd, stating, "No day of affliction passes over me without a day of ease passing over you, until we both arrive at a day that has no end, where the wrongdoers will be the losers."[4]

---

1. Qur'an 98:1
2. Qur'an 14:28
3. *Biḥār al-Anwār,* vol. 56, p. 223.
4. Ibid., vol. 48, p. 148.

Chapter Five

His Ordeal and Martyrdom

The sufferings and sorrows of Imam Mūsā b. Jaʿfar (peace be upon him) after the tragedy of Karbala were more painful and severe than those of the other Imams. Hārūn al-Rashīd watched over him closely but could not capture him, perhaps fearing that sending an army against him might lead to its defection to the Imam's side. The secretive work of the messengers made the authorities distrust even those closest to them. ʿAlī b. Yaqṭīn, Hārūn's minister, and his other minister Jaʿfar b. Muḥammad b. al-Ashʿath, were Shiites, as were some of his military leaders and key governors, who concealed their loyalty to the Ahl al-Bayt (peace be upon them).

Therefore, Hārūn decided to go to Medina himself to arrest the Imam, taking with him his special forces and a large group of poets, court scholars, advisors, and others. He also took millions of dinars stolen from the deprived, which he distributed among the people to buy their silence, particularly the tribal leaders and prominent opponents.

Thus, Hārūn went to Medina to arrest the greatest opponent of his usurping authority. Let's see what he did:

1. First, he spent several days meeting people and giving them generous gifts until he satisfied the bellies of the opposition, whose opposition was based on personal and private interests.

2. Second, he spread rumors against the enemies of the Sultan, enticing poets and court agents claiming to be religious scholars to praise the Sultan and issue fatwas forbidding fighting against him.

3. Third, he displayed his power to the people of Medina to prevent anyone from thinking of resisting him at this time.

4. When all conditions were set, Harun personally executed the final part of his conspiratorial plan. He went to the mosque of the

Messenger of Allah (peace be upon him and his family). Perhaps his presence coincided with prayer time when people, including Imam Mūsā b. Jafar (peace be upon him), would be present for prayer.

He then approached the Prophet's grave, greeted him, and said, "Peace be upon you, O Messenger of Allah, son of my uncle." His aim was to establish the legitimacy of his succession to the Prophet (peace be upon him and his family), to justify arresting the Imam (peace be upon him), but the Imam foiled this opportunity. He pushed through the crowd, approached the grave, and said to the astonishment of everyone, "Peace be upon you, O Messenger of Allah, peace be upon you, my grandfather."

If the Prophet is your uncle's son, O tyrant Sultan, and you claim the legitimacy of your authority based on your kinship to the Prophet, he is closer to me. He is my grandfather, and I am more deserving of his succession than you.

However, Hārūn then said, justifying his intention to arrest the Imam, "May my father and mother be sacrificed for you, O Messenger of Allah! I apologize to you for what I am determined to do. I want to arrest Mūsā b. Jaʿfar and imprison him because I fear he might incite a war among your nation, spilling their blood."[1]

The next day, he sent al-Faḍl b. al-Rabīʿ to arrest him while he was praying at the place of the Messenger of Allah (peace be upon him and his family). He was taken out of his house on two mules, each covered with a canopy, and each accompanied by cavalry. One took the road to Basra, and the other to Kufa to mislead people about his whereabouts. He was in the one that went to Basra. Hārūn ordered that he be handed over to ʿIsā b. Jaʿfar b. al-Manṣūr, who was in charge of Basra at the time. He remained imprisoned with him for a year.

Then ʿIsā wrote to Hārūn, "Take him from me and hand him over to whomever you wish, or I will release him. I have tried to find a reason against him, but I could not. I even listened to him when he

1. *Biḥār al-Anwār,* vol. 48, p. 213.

prayed, hoping he would curse me or you, but I only heard him pray for himself, asking for mercy and forgiveness. So, send someone to take him from me."

He was then transferred to the custody of al-Faḍl b. al-Rabīʿ in Baghdad, where he remained for a long time. Hārūn tried to persuade him on certain matters, but he refused. So Hārūn ordered him to be handed over to al-Faḍl b. Yaḥyā, who took him. Hārūn heard that he was being treated well and in comfort, so he sent Masrūr the servant to Baghdad urgently. He ordered him to investigate and if he found the news true, he was to hand one letter to ʿAbbās b. Muḥammad, ordering him to execute it, and another letter to Sindī b. Shāhak, instructing him to follow Abbas' orders.[1]

The historical narration continues to say:

"When Yaḥyā b. Khālid heard about it, he rode to al-Rashīd and entered through a different door than the one people usually enter from, until he came behind him without him noticing. Then he said, 'Turn to me, O Commander of the Faithful.' Al-Rashīd turned to him in fright. Yaḥyā said, 'Al-Faḍl is young, and I can handle what you want.' Al-Rashīd's face lit up with joy, and he turned to the people and said, 'Al-Faḍl had disobeyed me in something, so I cursed him. Now he has repented and returned to my obedience, so support him.' They said, 'We love whoever you love and hate whoever you hate. Now, we love.'

Then Yaḥyā b. Khālid left Hārūn and personally went to Baghdad with a letter. People were astonished by Yaḥyā's sudden arrival. Rumors spread about his sudden appearance, but Yaḥyā pretended to be there to address the city's affairs and the officials' performance. After spending a few days on these matters, he summoned Sindī b. Shāhak and conveyed the order to kill the Imam. Sindī carried out his order.

Mūsā (peace be upon him) asked Sindī at his death to bring a

---

1. Ibid., p. 233.

servant who resided near the house of ʿAbbās b. Muḥammad among the people of al-Qaṣab to wash him. This was done, and Mūsā also asked him to allow him to shroud him, but he refused, saying, 'We are a family whose women's dowries, pilgrimage expenses, and shrouds for our dead come from our own pure wealth. I have my shroud.'

When he died, the scholars and notable people of Baghdad, including al-Haytham b. ʿAdī and others, were present at his funeral to witness and testify that there were no signs of torture on him and that he had died a natural death. He was then taken and placed on the bridge in Baghdad, and it was announced, 'This is Mūsā b. Jaʿfar, who has died. Look at him.' People gathered to see him, even though he was dead.

A man from the Ṭālibiyīn told me that it was announced over him, 'This is Mūsā b. Jaʿfar, whom the Rāfiḍa claim will not die. Look at him now.' They looked at him. They carried him and buried him in the Quraysh cemetery, and his grave was placed next to a man from the Nawfaliyīn, named ʿIsā b. ʿAbdullah."[1]

According to historical reports, Imam al-Kāẓim (peace be upon him) maintained communication with his followers and supporters from prison, giving them instructions and addressing their political and jurisprudential issues.

We might wonder how he contacted them? Perhaps this communication occurred through supernatural means. However, many traditions clarify that most of the people in whose custody the Imam was imprisoned were believers in his Imamate. Despite the government's efforts to choose the harshest and most loyal jailers, even they witnessed his piety, extensive knowledge, and noble character, observing many miracles from him.

In the book *Biḥār Al-Anwār,* al-ʿĀmirī said: "Hārūn al-Rashīd sent a beautiful slave girl to Mūsā b. Jaʿfar to serve him in prison. He said,

---

1. *Biḥār al-Anwār,* vol. 48, p. 233, cited from *al-Ghayba* by al-Shaykh al-Ṭūsī, p. 22.

'Tell him, but you are pleased with your gifts.' I have no need for her or her kind." "Tell Harun: 'But you are happy with your gift'" I have no need for this maid or anyone like her."

Hārūn became furious and said, 'Return to him and tell him, 'We did not imprison you at your pleasure, nor did we take you with your consent. Leave the slave girl with him and go.' The servant returned and reported.

Hārūn then rose from his seat and sent a servant to inquire about her condition. They found her prostrate, worshipping her Lord, not raising her head, saying, 'Holy are You, Glory be to You.' Hārūn said, 'Mūsā b. Jaʿfar bewitched her with his magic; bring her to me.' He brought her and saw her trembling, her eyes fixed towards the sky. He asked, 'What has happened to you?' She said, 'This is the state of Mūsā b. Jaʿfar. I was standing by him while he was praying day and night. When he finished his prayer, he turned to me, glorifying and sanctifying Allah. I asked, 'My master, do you need anything I can provide?' He replied, 'What do I need from you?' I said, 'I was brought to you for your needs.' He asked, 'What about these?' I turned and saw a blooming garden I could not see the end of, filled with luxurious seats, beautiful servants I had never seen the like of, wearing green silk, crowns, pearls, and rubies, holding pitchers and napkins and all kinds of food. I fell prostrate until this servant raised me, and I found myself where I was.'

Hārūn said, 'You vile woman, you might have slept and dreamed this in your sleep?' She replied, 'No, my master, I saw this before I prostrated, and I prostrated because of that.'

al-Rashīd said, 'Take this vile woman away so that no one hears this from her.' She continued in prayer, saying, 'This is how I saw the righteous servant (alʿAbd al-Ṣāliḥ).' When asked about her words, she said, 'When I witnessed this matter, the maidens called me, 'O so-and-so, keep away from the righteous servant, so we can enter upon him. We are for him, not you.' She continued like this until she died, shortly before the death of Mūsā (peace be upon him).[1]

This is the honor of the Imam (peace be upon him) with Allah, and this is the fate of the tyrant al-Rashīd.

We ask Allah Almighty to make us among those who support His allies, disassociate from His enemies, and follow the path of the Imams of guidance from the family of Muḥammad (peace be upon him and his family). All praise is due to Allah, the Lord of the worlds.

1. *Biḥār al-Anwār,* vol. 48, p. 238-239.